The Management Guide to Understanding Behaviour

Kate Keenan

RAVETTE PUBLISHING

Published by Ravette Publishing Limited
P.O. Box 296
Horsham
West Sussex RH13 8FH
Telephone: (01403) 711443
Fax: (01403) 711554

Series Editor – Anne Tauté
Editor – Catriona Scott

Cover design – Jim Wire
Printing & Binding – Cox & Wyman Ltd.
Production – Oval Projects Ltd.

An Oval Project
produced for Ravette Publishing.

Cover – Some people cut the top off their
eggs, others pick the shell off bit by bit.
Both demonstrate different types of
behaviour.

Acknowledgement:
Peggy Dalton
Angela Summerfield

Contents

This book is dedicated to
those who would like to manage better
but are too busy to begin.

Understanding Behaviour

Understanding behaviour can be a bit of a problem. The main way people judge others is by observing their behaviour and coming to conclusions. But this is somewhat akin to judging the extent of an iceberg by its tip. As everyone knows, 90% of its structure is hidden beneath the surface. No-one knows exactly what is lurking in the ocean depths.

The behaviour that occasions most interest is problem behaviour. When people are behaving well, there is no necessity to explore the reasons for their behaviour. But when they are not, it forms a subject for endless speculation. Understanding what could be causing this can help considerably when coping with it.

This book attempts to throw some light on why people behave as they do, and examines many of the fascinating factors that govern behaviour; it gives you an insight into others' behaviour, and possibly even your own.

1. The Need to Understand Behaviour

Unless you understand behaviour – that is to say, what might be causing human beings to do certain things, you cannot begin to make sense of other people's actions. Even if you do, you cannot be certain that you are right. The ability to make a distinction between what you actually observe and what you infer from your observations is a major step in beginning to understand and attribute reasons for behaviour.

Not Observing Behaviour Objectively

It may appear obvious that if you are to understand behaviour you need to be able to observe it objectively, but people are remarkably adept at summing up other people's behaviour on very little evidence. They can develop complex opinions about others' personalities from one or two aspects of the behaviour they have observed. For example, someone may be thought to be 'friendly' simply because he paid attention to you; or 'obnoxious' because she contradicted you.

People are apt to confuse personality with behaviour. They tend to make judgements, apply labels, and only notice those aspects of behaviour which confirm their opinions about a particular person.

For example you may have heard it said:

- "He's got a personality problem."
- "She has the wrong attitude."
- "They're so set in their ways."

Being able to separate what people do from your opinion of them enables you to observe their behaviour objectively. This provides you with more reliable evidence from which you can begin to deduce why they might be behaving as they are.

Misinterpreting the Causes

Understanding the reasons for behaviour is not always straightforward. If you have not appreciated that it is difficult to interpret behaviour unless you know whether someone has acted intentionally or not, you could easily make the wrong assumptions.

For example, if you consider it to be a deliberate slight that an acquaintance walks straight past you without acknowledgement, you may decide to ignore him next time you meet.

On the other hand, if you think that your acquaintance's failure to acknowledge you was not deliberate because it was totally out of character, you might attribute the cause as preoccupation, and telephone to find out if there is a problem. Because you do not think he passed you by on purpose, you will look for an outside cause to explain the behaviour and be prepared to offer help.

You cannot know the reasons behind other people's behaviour; you can only observe what they do and then try to interpret it. If you believe that other people's behaviour is intentional, you will not take into account the range of possible reasons which could have caused it, so it will not occur to you to make allowances for their behaviour.

Yet because you are aware of the reasons behind what you do, when it comes to your own behaviour you will always expect others to believe that your own is unintentional and that you must have had a good reason for behaving in the way you did.

Misinterpreting behaviour by ascribing intention to it in the belief that people are fully in control of their actions, and not giving them the benefit of the doubt, is a major cause of misunderstanding behaviour.

Classifying Behaviour

Behaviour can be difficult to cope with because it is not always easy to classify in a sensible fashion. In general terms, there are three distinct categories of behaviour which offer an insight into why people are functioning in a certain way:

1. **Basic Behaviour**. This is a combination of innate behaviour, which has to do with individual temperament, and learned behaviour which everyone acquires as they grow up and which helps them to function in the world.
2. **Distressed Behaviour**. This is behaviour which people may exhibit when they find themselves in adverse circumstances.
3. **Needful Behaviour**. This is behaviour which reflects people's deepest emotional needs.

Appreciating that behaviour can be driven by these different forces goes a long way towards understanding why people behave as they do.

Summary: Focussing on Behaviour

When dealing with all forms of behaviour, it can be difficult to focus solely on the behaviour itself without your own subjective interpretations getting in the way. To understand behaviour you need to focus on **what** is happening before you make judgements about **why** it is happening. Once you are able to take an objective view of behaviour, you stand a good chance of understanding it.

Questions to Ask Yourself

Think about your attitude to behaviour and how you react to it, and answer the following questions:

- Do I sometimes find it difficult to remain objective when observing behaviour?
- Do I tend to judge people on one or two aspects of their behaviour?
- Do I find it difficult to separate people's behaviour from their personalities?
- Do I assume that people know what they are doing?
- Do I tend to believe that people do things deliberately rather than unintentionally?
- Do I ascribe motives to other people that I would never ascribe to myself?
- Do I sometimes fail to interpret behaviour correctly?

If you have answered 'Yes' to some or all of these questions, you may need to assess how well you understand behaviour.

You Will Be Doing Better If...

★ You appreciate that it can be difficult to remain objective about behaviour.

★ You try not to jump to conclusions about people's personalities before you have evidence to explain their behaviour.

★ You try to see people's behaviour as separate from their personalities.

★ You appreciate that people are not necessarily in control of their behaviour.

★ You avoid thinking that someone has done something deliberately until you find out more.

★ You consider some of the reasons why people could be behaving as they are.

★ You recognize that interpreting behaviour is more complex than it seems.

2. Basic Behaviour

To understand behaviour you need to appreciate that human beings are an amalgam of their experiences and their character. This affects their perceptions and leads them to behave in uniquely personal ways. Therefore no one person can see things in the same way as another, nor will he or she necessarily behave in the same way even if they do.

If all behaviour were exemplary and people were kind, honest, well-balanced, consistent, helpful, supportive, open, sympathetic, caring and concerned, there would be little need to understand behaviour. But often it is not, so there is a great deal to gain by looking a little more deeply into what influences people to behave in the way they do.

Behaviour stems from three basic sources: **nature** (heredity), **nurture** (environment) and **gender** (sexual identity), all of which directly influence the way people behave.

Nature

Nature provides people with their disposition, in the form of temperament and personality, which prompts them to perceive the world in their own unique way and predisposes them to behave in individual styles.

Temperament

Everyone is born with a set of inherent characteristics. These include inherited genes and the effects of prenatal conditions, and it is innate temperament that defines in people their individual moods, sensitivities and levels of energy. People are born with these qualities and can do little to change them. They form some of the building blocks from which their distinct personality and individuality develops.

Personality

Five main groups of related traits make up the basic aspects of personality. These indicate the degree to which people are:

- **Emotionally Stable**. Whether you tend to be nervous or calm; vulnerable or hardy; insecure or secure. This also includes whether you are anxious, hostile, morose, self-conscious, impulsive, etc.
- **Extrovert**. Whether you tend to be reticent or sociable; shy or talkative; inhibited or spontaneous. This also involves the extent to which you are warm, gregarious, assertive, active, excitement-seeking, etc.
- **Conscientious**. Whether you tend to be careless or careful; undependable or reliable; negligent or

conscientious. This also embraces the extent to which you are competent, orderly, dutiful, achievement-orientated, self-disciplined, methodical, etc.

- **Agreeable**. Whether you tend to be more irritable than good-natured; ruthless or soft-hearted; selfish or selfless. This includes being trusting, compliant, altruistic, modest, straight-forward, tender-hearted, etc.

- **Open to Experience**. Whether you tend to be more conventional than original; unadventurous or daring; conservative or liberal. This includes being imaginative, creative, artistic, sympathetic, open-minded, etc.

These basic components of personality predispose people to behave in certain ways, whatever they might wish – like the frog and the scorpion. In this tale, both wish to cross a fast-flowing river. The scorpion asks to be carried across by the frog, who is reluctant to do so, fearing he will be stung. The scorpion assures the frog he will be safe because if he stung him they would both drown, so they set off. But halfway across, the scorpion stings the frog. With his dying breath the frog asks, "Why?" to which the scorpion replies, "Because it's my nature".

Thus, the inherent factors which determine individual personality or nature, have a direct bearing on basic behaviour.

Nurture

Nobody is born with all the behaviour they demonstrate. People learn from their surroundings and develop the way they behave in the course of growing up. What sort of experiences they have had, and how they have been conditioned to react, tend to make a considerable difference to how they behave as adults.

Learning and Conditioning

As people grow up, their responses are conditioned by trial and error. They rapidly learn to respond in certain ways, like Pavlov's little dogs who were taught to expect food to turn up every time a bell rang. Responses are often influenced by what has proved effective in the past. During their lives, people learn to respond to and are conditioned by various factors such as:

- **Parental influence**. This plays a major part in modelling initial behaviour. Love, affection and interest usually produce feelings of security and confidence. Indifference or outright rejection may provoke people to behave in ways – even as extreme as violence – which will gain them attention.
- **Friends, work colleagues, teachers or popular idols**. These can provide influential role models. When there are no obvious figureheads, trying to

achieve specific objectives may prove more difficult because there are no guidelines to follow.

- **Day-to-day activities.** These continuously condition and modify behaviour. Experiences gained at an early age tend to be longer-lasting and can permeate behaviour more pervasively.

People go on learning, adapting, and shaping their behaviour throughout their lives – the conditioning process never stops.

Reinforcement

While learning, people often discover what is acceptable and what is not by being rewarded for good actions and punished when they overstep the mark. Behaviour is strengthened by this reinforcement. Indeed, once the behaviour is in place, it will often be maintained even if it is only reinforced a fraction of the time. Thus with Pavlov's dogs, despite the food being withheld, at the ringing of the bell they continued for months to lick their chops in anticipation.

Once people have learned to adapt to or avoid certain situations, they may continue to behave in the same way long after they need to because nothing has happened to prevent them from behaving that way – they have simply formed a habit.

Gender

Gender is the third factor to play a significant part in determining basic behaviour.

Most people are aware that gender makes a difference to their nature, but it may be less apparent that gender also conditions them because of the way they are nurtured.

Children are more often than not raised by females. Both sexes are initially influenced by this female role model and conditioned in a supportive and emotional way. However, at a critical point in their youth, boys face a dramatic change when they are introduced to the male role model where developing self-confidence, being courageous and winning are pre-requisites for success. Under the male influence boys quickly learn that showing their emotions is not acceptable.

Meanwhile girls' behaviour is fostered and developed under a continuous female influence, in the expectation that they will marry, have children and be the providers of nurture for everyone within their sphere of influence.

This fundamental conditioning means that each sex tends to work from a completely different set of behavioural rules. Women are allowed, if not encouraged, to be dependent and emotional, while men are usually required to behave rationally and independently.

Behavioural Responses

By and large, nature, nurture and gender work together to produce reasonable behaviour which enables people to live comfortably within the conventions of society. But some behaviour can be disruptive. Spotting what triggers this can be useful.

Reinforced Behaviour

The reinforcement of learned responses can produce ingrained and unproductive patterns of behaviour. For instance:

- If people often get their own way by having a temper-tantrum, or bullying, they soon learn that this is a good method of achieving their ends. Every time they succeed, the behaviour is reinforced, making it more likely that they will do it again.

- If people are told repeatedly that they are not capable of doing what is required, or that they do not measure up to what is expected, they learn to doubt their abilities, lose confidence and cease trying altogether.

- If people are badly let down, they will hesitate to trust others again. Should this occur more than once with one person, or once with a number of people, they will inevitably learn never to trust anyone again.

- If people are criticized or reprimanded for their work no matter what the quality, they will soon feel there is little point in making any effort. They will simply decide that it is not worth taking time or trouble to do good work at all.

The more people's negative behaviour is reinforced, the more it becomes entrenched, and the less easy it is to change.

Self-fulfilling Prophecies

If people have in mind certain outcomes (whether they are good ones or bad ones), it is more likely these predictions will occur and, by doing so, become self-fulfilling prophecies.

- **Living up to expectations**. If people are expected and encouraged to perform well, they usually do. If they are told they are useless, they tend to expect nothing of themselves.

- **Learned helplessness**. If people are prevented from controlling their own actions or influencing their circumstances, they tend to believe that they cannot achieve anything, so they usually do not.

- **Positive control**. If people believe that control of their lives comes largely from their own efforts, they will strive to get on in life. Those who develop strong inner resources usually achieve more because they are convinced that they will do so.

When people act on the forecasts that they or others make, it is an odds-on bet that these will come true. Depending on experience and conditioning, people will either be positive or negative about their expectations. So whether they are looking for a good or a bad outcome, they are rarely disappointed.

Summary: Understanding People

Everyone brings an individual personality and unique set of learned behaviour to any situation. Appreciating that there is an interaction between inherited factors and those acquired through experience, helps you to understand why different people act differently.

It is the combination of nature, nurture and gender which determines how people behave.

Questions to Ask Yourself

Think about whether you understand behaviour and ask yourself the following questions:

- Do I realize that people's temperament and personality incline them to behave in certain ways?
- Am I aware that there are a huge number of personality traits which influence behaviour?
- Do I recognize the part that experience and conditioning play in developing behaviour?
- Do I understand that when behaviour is reinforced it is more likely to continue?
- Do I appreciate that behaviour can be affected by self-fulfilling prophecies?
- Do I understand that behaviour is determined by a combination of nature, nurture and gender?

You Will Be Doing Better If...

★ You appreciate that people are predisposed to behave in certain ways.

★ You realize that behaviour is influenced by a wide range of personality traits.

★ You recognize that conditioning plays a large part in determining the way people behave.

★ You understand that reinforcement causes learned responses to become habitual.

★ You realize that self-fulfilling prophecies may govern people's behaviour.

★ You know that it is the interaction of nature, nurture and gender which determines behaviour.

3. Distressed Behaviour

In the ordinary course of their lives, people experience distressing circumstances which can have a deleterious effect on their behaviour. You need to understand why.

Many of these are of a temporary nature and, however unpleasant, can be got over in time. But sometimes they can linger and have lasting repercussions.

Distressing experiences may condition behaviour more or less permanently; for example, an unsupported or thoroughly unhappy childhood. Serious misfortune, such as bereavement or divorce, can severely affect behaviour for a time, but by and large, most people recover from these events.

In general, distressed behaviour comes from two sources:

- **External circumstances** which have a dramatic impact on people's lives.
- **Internal conditions** which have an insidious effect on people's states of mind.

External Circumstances

Most people perform well when they feel that life is controllable and predictable; that events present a challenge and can be coped with successfully. But sometimes things that happen, and the circumstances in which they find themselves, can overwhelm people and cause serious changes in their behaviour.

Workaday Stress

Stress is experienced when people feel events are not under their control, are unpredictable or confront the limits of their capabilities. The sorts of situations which can cause undue distress are:

- **Difficulties at work**. A mismatch between the demands of the work and the level of individual capability can lead to a feeling of inadequacy and cause performance to deteriorate.
- **Domestic and personal problems**. A health problem, stormy relationships or family tragedy, are events which can occupy someone's mind to the exclusion of everything else. If people are absorbed by such problems, they will not be able to concentrate on other things which demand their attention.
- **Excessive responsibilities**. A need to meet stringent standards and tight deadlines puts pressure on people to take on too many responsibilities in order to fulfil their obligations. The fear of not achieving what is required can be stultifying and inhibit performance.

The same stressful circumstances do not trigger the same reactions in people, but everyone tends to be affected in some way or another.

Post Traumatic Stress

Traumatic events – i.e. those which are outside the usual range of human experience, such as being involved in (or even simply witnessing) accidents, disasters, assaults or serious threat to life or limb can inflict stress of a specific sort.

Responses to dramatic events vary, but there is one common syndrome of behaviour everyone demonstrates. At first, people feel dazed and disorganized and even unaware of any injury sustained. Next, they become passive and unable to initiate actions, but will follow orders. Finally, they become anxious, apprehensive and have difficulties concentrating. They may also have emotional reactions to anything which they associate with the event. People differ greatly in how quickly and completely they recover. Simply knowing about post traumatic stress allows you to understand the behaviour and make allowances for it.

Alcohol and Drugs

Alcohol and drugs can seriously affect behaviour. In the main, these substances are used in an attempt to cope with adverse circumstances. Some deeper underlying problem is made more tolerable by using them. Some substances depress reactions and temporarily blot out the problem, while others stimulate people to keep going or give a transitory boost to confidence.

Problems associated with alcohol and/or drugs are rather like a Russian doll. You open the outer one, but find there is another one inside and another inside that. The outside one is synonymous with the problem, but does not explain the cause which led to the use of alcohol and/or drugs in the first place, and which have since become a problem in themselves. It may be the second, sixth or tenth doll which needs to be opened in order to expose the underlying problem which could fully explain the behaviour.

Internal Conditions

People's mental state can be affected by internal conditions and sometimes produce physical chemical change. The most common distress comes from:

Anxiety

Most people feel anxious and tense when faced with threatening or stressful situations, and such feelings are a normal reaction to stress. But when someone is unduly anxious in situations that other people handle without difficulty, it can become a real problem.

Someone who suffers from acute anxiety lives each day in a state of tension. The individual feels uneasy or apprehensive much of the time and tends to overreact to even mild stresses. He or she worries about potential problems and finds it difficult to concentrate and make decisions. "Did I foresee all the possible consequences?" "Did I remember to switch the lights out?" Whatever the cause (early conditioning or experience, or a possible chemical imbalance which prevents the anxiety from being blocked when it is not an appropriate reaction to have), you need to understand that, however hard they try, people may not be able to control this behaviour.

Depression

Few people live their lives on an even keel all the time. It is not unnatural to feel despair, or become depressed and tearful, as a result of an upsetting or disturbing event – such as the ending of a relationship or failure in some form. But sometimes depression can become chronic, either because of the long-term circumstances in which people find themselves, and about which they can do nothing, or possibly because the chemistry in the brain is preventing emotions from being appropriately regulated. This means they are unable to lift themselves out of depression, which in turn makes them feel even more depressed. It is a vicious circle.

When in this state, people often find it hard to concentrate, feel that it is futile to make any effort to change their circumstances, and often believe that the future is hopeless.

No amount of exhortation to 'snap out of it' has any effect. All that can be done is to be understanding and compassionate.

Spotting the Signs

Being aware of some of the causes of distressed behaviour is a good starting point, but you need to spot the signs which can signal that people are having problems. These usually take the form of changes in behaviour.

Signs of Distressed Behaviour

If people's behaviour changes for the worse for any length of time, it is a fairly clear indication that something is not right. Realizing that people are behaving in ways which are different from usual requires you to be familiar with how they normally behave. Some warning signs are more obvious than others. For example:

- Turning up late, when previously always prompt for everything.
- Being withdrawn and apathetic, when formerly outgoing and energetic.
- Having angry outbursts over trivial things, when usually reasonably even-tempered.
- Exhibiting a scruffy appearance, when habitually immaculate.
- Presenting slip-shod work when normally meticulous and painstaking.
- Becoming forgetful and failing to pay attention to detail when formerly punctilious.
- Being muddled and confused when previously well-organized.
- Manifesting an all-pervasive sadness when generally light-hearted and bright.

All these signs signal some form of personal trouble, often of a temporary nature, but sometimes leading to a permanent state. It is natural to interpret such changes as a loss of interest in work or sheer laziness, but if you do, you could be failing to understand the real reason behind the behaviour which is causing these signs of distress.

Signs of Alcoholic Behaviour

Less easy to spot, because it does not always show itself as being so different from normal, and builds up over a long period, is alcoholic behaviour. The sorts of signs which should cause concern are:

- Performance which is unpredictable or inconsistent. Some days the individual output is intense, at other times negligible, so you find it difficult to schedule work or rely on its delivery.

- 'Accidents' which occur rather too frequently to be accidental and which are inadequately justified, so you never know what to expect next.

- Changes in mood which are difficult to explain. On some days the moods are good humoured and sociable, on others sulky and argumentative (even changing from one hour to the next) so everyone is affected by the prevailing temperament.

- Absences for minor ailments such as 'a flu bug' or a 'tummy ache' or for no given reason. Sometimes it is the odd day off – often a Monday – so you are never sure of regular attendance.

- Insistent invitations to have a drink at lunchtime or after work, so you feel you are being press-ganged to join in.

It can be difficult to identify when people are using alcohol to excess, because they are usually very good at hiding it. You have to piece together a jigsaw of information made up of the behavioural clues you have observed, and even remarks made by others.

One sign may not be enough to cause you to notice anything specifically untoward, but more than two should begin to alert you to the possible association with alcohol. But care needs to be taken in attributing this as the cause because some of these symptoms can also indicate long-term problems of a different kind (such as being systematically bullied at work, or even another form of addiction like gambling or drugs).

It is is vital therefore that you weigh all the evidence before drawing any conclusions, and you may need to get expert advice.

Summary: Being Aware

There are many reasons for distressed behaviour. People react differently to circumstances and it is not always easy to establish the cause. But being aware of some of the causes makes it easier for you to be more tolerant of what you observe and more capable of understanding it.

Questions to Ask Yourself

Think about how distress may affect the way people behave and answer the following questions:

- Do I recognize that people usually feel stressed when they feel that events are no longer under their control?
- Do I understand that trauma can have serious effects?
- Do I appreciate that alcohol is often used as a prop in order to cope?
- Do I understand how anxiety and depression can alter behaviour?
- Do I appreciate that changes in behaviour may often indicate distress?
- Do I usually notice if someone behaves in an uncharacteristic way?

You Will Be Doing Better If...

★ You are aware of the effect workaday stress can have on people's behaviour.

★ You understand the devastating effect of post-traumatic stress.

★ You appreciate that anxiety can cause behaviour to degenerate.

★ You realize that depression can cause people to find it difficult to cope with their lives.

★ You recognize that there is often an underlying problem which causes people to take alcohol or drugs.

★ You notice when someone's behaviour is different from usual.

★ You understand that changes in behaviour can signal that someone is severely distressed.

4. Needful Behaviour

People's needs are invariably reflected in their behaviour. Everybody has needs, such as the need for emotional reciprocation or recognition of achievement, which they seek to satisfy in order to achieve their potential. People are usually capable of satisfying their needs, but when they are not, they may act out their frustration by playing psychological games.

Such expressions of need usually affect other people more than the person behaving in this way, and may not even be recognized by those initiating it. It is important to understand that certain types of behaviour, however irritating or aggravating, may simply be reflecting need.

Identifying Need

What people consistently say and do often provides an indication as to what deep-seated but unfulfilled needs are present. Most people have an idea of the sort of person they would like to be.

But, when there is a discrepancy between the person they would like to be and how they actually regard themselves, they will demonstrate needs which mirror the gap that needs filling.

For example:

- **A need for constant reassurance**. This need to be bolstered shows up in a tendency to say things like "I'm no good at this" or "Is this alright?".
- **A need to be needed**. This is a basic desire to make life more meaningful by seeking out and being surrounded by dependent others.
- **A need for attention**. This denotes a need to be noticed or admired. It often shows up as a tendency to show off and to take centre stage in any situation.
- **A need for approval**. This may be expressing a need for love and affection and is often exhibited by constantly trying to please.

These are only a very few of the range of needs which you may identify and which indicate some of the deep-seated needs in people that are not being met. You cannot expect to uncover their cause, nor understand their origins, but you can come to terms with the fact that the overall need to be regarded positively by someone else is a basic one which people seek to satisfy in whatever way they can.

You can often help people reduce their needful behaviour by making them feel that they are valued. When people feel valued, they are more likely to function positively and their underlying needs will therefore become less dominant and less apparent.

Recognizing Role-Playing

People whose deep-seated needs are not being met can act out their frustration by spending a great deal of their working and social lives manipulating others in an attempt to fulfil those needs. They can adopt various positions in life which colour all other behaviour. This usually means that the range of their actions is limited and that they can become trapped in behavioural ruts.

The two most commonly adopted are:

- **Being a Victim**. This behaviour leads people to blame circumstances or other people for the fact that they are not what they think they should be. It absolves them of any blame for their actions, or lack of them. They like to moan about things preventing them from achieving a goal, "If only I had more time"; and to something that has gone wrong, the cry is "Look what you've gone and made me do."

- **Being a Victor**. This behaviour leads people to convince themselves that they are equal to or better than anyone else by a series of small personal victories which take the form of "I'm the king of the castle." They like to let you know how successful they have been, usually at the expense of someone else. To a comment such as, "This works well", the reply will be "It was my idea to do it".

Those who take on these 'life-positions' tend to get trapped into a form of role-playing, displaying patterns of behaviour which can become ingrained and automatic and almost always lead to bad feelings, acrimony and ill will. This behaviour often manifests itself in little acts into which you can easily be drawn if you are caught unawares. For instance:

The Victim's role:

- **'The packed lunch.'** In this scenario, the star of the show is the packed lunch, which enables the player to insist on working through the lunch break, rather than going out, as you do, for a sandwich. During this time, the player is busy answering telephones and taking messages. On your return from lunch, the player complains bitterly, albeit righteously, about the amount of work done, thus effectively making you feel guilty, even though you never asked the player to do this in the first place.
- **'Yes, but...'** In this scenario, the player tells of a problem in such a way as to evince your sympathy and draws you into all the details and issues involved. When you offer practical or sensible solutions, any of which would alleviate the problem, you are consistently met with "Yes, but..." so that you feel you are really no help at all.

The Victor's role:

- **'You shouldn't have done that.'** In this scenario, you have either done or are doing something which requires a great deal effort, and the player tells you what you should be doing or should have done. This makes you justify your actions but leads you to doubt your own judgement.
- **'Aren't I clever!?'** The player either succeeds in outwitting someone by devious means and relating the triumph with relish, or gets their oar in first, in order to demonstrate their superiority or parity. You are sucked into collusion either as a captive audience or as a passive participant. You are then left exasperated and exhausted with the effort of withholding your true opinion which would have involved openly taking issue or condoning the action.

These and similar play-acts signal some form of need above and beyond the kind generally expressed by people trying to accommodate personal needs.

It is easy to dismiss those who behave as Victims or Victors as people who are either hard-done-by or revel in being know-it-alls, but if you do, you could be failing to understand what prompts the behaviour. Playing games supports and validates their chosen position. Without their roles, many people would be completely lost.

If you can recognize the performance by the script, you will know that you are in the middle of a scene from a melodrama which is essential to others' security. It is helpful to understand that this behaviour is prompted by a requirement to reinforce individual life positions which themselves arise from an attempt to cope with deep-seated needs.

Summary: Discerning Needful Behaviour

People can get themselves locked into a set of demotivating or destructive behaviour patterns which reinforce and emphasize their needs. They get bogged down in behavioural ruts often because they lack a range of behaviour which would enable them to cope.

Manifestations of needful behaviour are generally a cry for support rather than a search for an answer, and frequently the behaviour is trying to provoke your involvement even though the method seems to suggest the opposite.

Knowing what the signs can be covering makes it possible to accept that some behaviour may not be all that it seems.

Questions to Ask Yourself

Think about how people's needs could affect their behaviour and answer the following questions:

- Am I aware that people often express their deep-seated needs through their behaviour?
- Do I appreciate that everybody needs to feel valued?
- Do I understand that 'role-playing' is a pattern of behaviour that demonstrates unfulfilled needs?
- Do I recognize those who have chosen to see themselves as Victims and Victors?
- Do I understand that much needful behaviour is a cry for help?

You Will Be Doing Better If...

- ★ You are aware that some behaviour indicates deep-seated needs that are not being satisfied.
- ★ You realize that everyone needs to feel valued.
- ★ You know that some people need to be needed more than others.
- ★ You appreciate that when people are 'role-playing' they are reaffirming their beliefs about themselves.
- ★ You understand that demonstrating needful behaviour can be a cry for help.

5. Coping With Behaviour

Most people's behaviour does not affect the way they carry on doing what is required of them. It is when their behaviour has a detrimental effect on their performance that you need to consider how you will cope with it.

When handling problem behaviour you have to be objective, and you need to divorce the behaviour itself from the personality of the person caught up in it. Remind yourself that it is the behaviour that should be concerning you, not the individual's personality.

Evaluating Behaviour

Whether someone's aberrant behaviour has been prompted by external or internal causes, it helps to evaluate how this is affecting their lives.

If someone has had a serious shock to the system, such as a bereavement, or being made redundant, it is reasonable behaviour to be extremely unhappy and depressed for some time and to find it difficult to control the emotions. It is also quite natural to go on 'a bender' to try to blot out the immediate pain and anxiety. Serious problems arise, however, if this behaviour continues for a considerable time. Thus, if someone is numbed by grief or goes on drinking heavily long after the shock of loss should have worn off, some longer-term problems are likely to be building up which could affect their behaviour permanently.

While it is not possible to put a limit on how long people should display inappropriate behaviour, a very drawn out or extreme reaction would indicate that the person is not able to handle the situation and probably needs help. So before you try to cope with the behaviour, you need to attempt to assess whether it is attributable to distress of some sort or to deep-seated emotional needs.

Helping People to Cope

Having identified that someone's behaviour is causing problems, your main interest is to help the person to cope. This is best done by talking and, more importantly, listening. When you do this you need to:

- Indicate the precise changes in behaviour you have noticed and not your conclusions: "I'm concerned that you aren't meeting your targets" rather than "I think your work has gone downhill."
- Ask for an explanation, one that is not an accusation. "Is there any reason why you don't seem to be getting things done on time?" rather than "Why aren't you getting things done on time?"

- Listen to the answer and reflect back what was said so that people can consider whether the reason they have given is in fact the real one. "So you're saying that it's because you're unfamiliar with the new machine that you are late in delivering?" or "So the fact that your cat has just died is causing you difficulty in keeping your mind on the job?"

- Get people to generate various options or courses of action to ameliorate their difficulties. "What would you think about asking for training on the new machine?" "What might you do to prevent yourself feeling lonely without your cat?"

If you indicate your concern and the fact you have noticed that things are not right, people are more likely to discuss their behaviour. Until you ask questions and listen to the answers you cannot possibly get closer to the root cause.

Initially you may not have realized the seriousness of the situation, or not appreciated that the person is unable to face the facts him or herself. For example, it may emerge that the one who has lost his or her job is not qualified for anything else; or that the cat was the sole companion and had been so for 18 years – half the individual's own life.

By talking and listening, you can help people to get a better understanding of what could be causing their distress. You can also decide whether an individual needs:

- **Advice**. Providing useful suggestions about practical courses of action may help them to see a way forward and get going again.
- **Reassurance**. Reminding someone of his or her talents and strengths will boost confidence and help restore a sense of worth.
- **Sympathy**. Lending a sympathetic ear and encouraging someone to talk could be all that is needed to help an individual to face up to something he or she would rather avoid.

It may be that in certain situations there is very little practical help you can give, but one of the most supportive things you can do is to notice, acknowledge and respect whatever it is that affects a person to such a degree that it transforms their behaviour.

Helping Yourself to Cope

When behaviour can be attributed to deep-seated needs, you will be banging your head against a brick wall if you try to make someone aware of it, or try to change it.

It is vital to understand that people who seek constant reinforcement are locked into a pattern of behaviour and even if from time to time they seem to get out of it, at the first sign of daily life not going smoothly they will usually revert to it. Any suggestion that their behaviour is not appropriate will usually meet with solid resistance. Unlike coping with distressed behaviour, the desire to help may actually be counter-productive.

The desire to help people with deep-seated needs can be so strong that you may find yourself endlessly trying to make up for the emotional deficiencies in their lives by trying to provide a continuous drip-feed of comfort and support. But it is never enough. You will not be able to help and nothing you could do would satisfy them. Often all that happens is that you get weighed down by those who have chosen to see themselves as victims, and aggravated by those who feel the need to see themselves as victors. But most of all, you can end up feeling that the fault is yours and that if only you could give more, the person would stop being so needful.

To prevent being sucked into an emotional 'black hole' and drained of your energies, you can employ one of three strategies to cope with needful behaviour. You can either accommodate it, pass it on to someone qualified to deal with it, or avoid it altogether:

1. **Accommodating it**. Accommodating needful behaviour means learning to live with it. Either you take no notice of moods or attention seeking, or you develop a quick line in cheerful responses which deflects the behaviour.

2. **Passing it on**. Advising someone to seek professional help in the form of counselling or medical treatment is the most constructive way of coping with their behaviour. But unfortunately this is a course only open to you if the individual hints that he or she would not be averse to receiving help or in some way suggests an acknowledgment that there could be a problem.

3. **Avoiding it**. Choosing to avoid becoming embroiled is not the coward's way out. It can often be a good way of dealing with it, for once you refuse to play the game, it becomes less easy for others to do so because they no longer have a playmate. Walking away from needful behaviour may in fact be the only sensible course to take.

People do not generally intend to behave in difficult ways, and most of the time they are not really aware they are doing so. This means their behaviour can cause you more pain than it does them, so it is up to you to choose the method of coping with it that best suits you. For a tolerant person or one who feels especially committed to an individual, accommodating the conduct may be the obvious choice. But for someone less patient or less involved, steering clear of it could be the only option. And even if you do not choose to do so immediately, it is certainly a last resort.

Summary: Taking Action

Helping people to come to terms with what could be causing their difficult behaviour needs to be tackled sensitively and carefully if you are not to be accused of manipulating people and interfering in their lives.

When people's behaviour indicates distress, encouraging them to talk may bring about an understanding of the reasons behind their behaviour. It often enables them to pinpoint the root cause.

When role-playing indicates that deep-seated needs are responsible, you need to focus on the behaviour, not how you feel about the individual displaying it. You can then choose to live with it, deflect it or turn your back on it, all of which are equally valid methods of coping with it.

Questions to Ask Yourself

Think about coping with behaviour and answer the following questions:

- ▲ Am I aware that if people continue to show signs of distress for a long time, their behaviour may become permanently affected?
- ▲ Do I try to divorce my feelings for the person from the behaviour that he or she is exhibiting?
- ▲ Do I talk things over with people to find out what they think their problems may be?
- ▲ Am I prepared to give people practical advice when it is needed?
- ▲ Do I give people sympathy?
- ▲ Am I willing and able in some circumstances to accommodate needful behaviour?
- ▲ Do I walk away from behaviour when I feel it is too difficult to cope with?

You Will Be Doing Better If...

★ You recognize that continued reactions to situations may permanently affect behaviour.

★ You help people to cope by talking and listening to them.

★ You give people practical advice to help them to help themselves.

★ You sympathize with people and reassure them.

★ You are prepared to accommodate needful behaviour in certain circumstances.

★ You avoid behaviour that could cause you more difficulties that you can cope with.

★ You know you have a choice in the way you deal with needful behaviour.

6. Your Behaviour

It is all very well understanding more about difficult behaviour, and what could be causing it, but there is always the possibility it could be your own behaviour which is contributing more than its fair share to the situation.

You need to consider yourself part of the equation. It could be, for instance, that you are only seeing what you want to see, like the proud mother watching her son quick-marching to his own pace in the parade, who remarked "Everyone's out of step but our Willy". It may be you who are not in step with other people.

Your Personality

It is very difficult to see yourself in the same way as others see you. If you sometimes feel that you are desperately misunderstood, it could be that some aspects of your personality are to blame. You may need to take a long look at yourself and analyse how your disposition is influencing your behaviour.

By making an effort to face up to your nature, or perhaps discussing it with a kindred spirit, you are able to examine your inherent behaviour and perhaps begin to understand where you could modify certain aspects so that things will run more smoothly for you.

Your Conditioning

The nurturing you received in early life and your subsequent experience will have conditioned you to get what you want and shaped your responses; sometimes for the good and possibly sometimes for the worse.

You may be habitually reinforcing certain learned responses or you may be a martyr to your own self-fulfilling prophecies – both of which are causing you to behave in a certain way. You could even find yourself enacting some form of needful behaviour when you are up against the odds.

By becoming aware of how your conditioning colours your behaviour, you can start to modify it. For instance, if you find yourself saying, "I can't do that" because you lack faith in your ability, changing it to "I'll have a go" will extend your range of behaviour.

Never forget that you always have the power to change your behaviour. And once you change it, and it is reinforced, it will in turn become a habit.

The Way You See Things

When interpreting any situation in which you find yourself, you will be drawing on the many different ideas and assumptions you have formed during your life. So how you assess your behaviour may not necessarily tally with how others view it. For example:

- You think you are being determined, but others see you as stubborn or ruthless.
- You think you are authoritative, but others perceive you as bossy and domineering.

You may know your own intentions, but all people can see is your behaviour, and you need to be aware that they will interpret it in their own terms.

The Way You Behave

The way you behave will almost certainly affect the way others behave. It can sometimes be unnerving to realize that it is your behaviour that may have caused someone else to react in a certain way.

You will generally experience difficulties if you behave in one way but expect others to behave in another. For example:

- If you expect people to come in on time, but are persistently late yourself, you cannot really blame them if they take a cavalier attitude to time-keeping.
- If you expect people to work to rigorous standards, but make little attempt to comply with them yourself, people will be less inclined to make the effort.

The upshot is that your own behaviour has a much greater influence on everyone else than you may have ever understood, and it is this which can often induce others to behave as they do.

Summary: Knowing Yourself

Understanding behaviour in general is a prerequisite to understanding your own and anyone else's. Being aware of what parts your personality and conditioning play in governing how you behave, means that you stand a better chance of doing so.

This is not always a guarantee of success and sometimes you can get it wrong. But you can use your knowledge to analyse your behaviour and make more sense of other people's.

Questions to Ask Yourself

Think about your own behaviour and answer the following questions:

- Do I appreciate that my personality can have a bearing on my behaviour?
- Do I realize my responses are affected by my conditioning?
- Am I aware that the intention behind my behaviour might be interpreted differently by others?
- Do I behave in the way I expect others to behave?
- Do I realize that if my behaviour is not productive and positive I can change it?
- Am I conscious of how much my behaviour can affect other people's behaviour?

You Will Be Doing Better If...

- ★ You try to understand the effect of your personality on your behaviour.

- ★ You acknowledge that your conditioning affects how you behave.

- ★ You recognize that others might interpret your behaviour in a different way from that which you intended.

- ★ You try to ensure you do not expect behaviour of others that you do not practise yourself.

- ★ You realize that you can always change your behaviour if you are dissatisfied with it.

- ★ You are well aware of the influence your behaviour can have on others.

Check List for Understanding Behaviour

If you are finding that understanding behaviour is proving less easy than you thought, consider whether it is because you have failed to take account of one or more of the following aspects:

Basic Behaviour

If people behave in ways which you find difficult, it may be that you have not come to terms with what underlies basic behaviour. You may be failing to understand that behaviour stems from the interaction of temperament, personality and conditioning. Nature and nurture work together to determine how people behave, and produce infinite combinations.

Distressed Behaviour

If you are too busy to pay attention to other people's behaviour, you may not be spotting the clues which indicate that something is wrong. It could be that events have overwhelmed them, and that you have not understood the dramatic effects this can have on their behaviour. Acknowledging that anxiety and depression can affect how people behave, also gives you good reason for their actions and moods.

Needful Behaviour

If you find yourself unable to explain someone's behaviour it may be that you are not appreciating that it could be due to the effects of emotional deprivation. Perhaps you have not spotted the clues which signify that people are playing psychological games as a way of expressing their deep-seated needs. If you wake up to what is happening, you will be able to deal with it.

Coping with Behaviour

If you find yourself constantly frustrated and troubled by people's behaviour, it may be that you have become too deeply involved to look at it objectively. It could be that you are trying to help those who cannot be helped, or have not spent enough time helping others to help themselves. Or you may not yet have understood that it is behaviour which you must try to handle rather than the personality.

Your Behaviour

If you are puzzled by people's reactions to you, perhaps you are not taking account of the impact that your behaviour can have upon others' behaviour. Having a proper understanding of basic behaviour will help you to come to terms with your own and that of other people.

The Benefits of Understanding Behaviour

Understanding human behaviour is an infinitely enriching activity. To do it well you need to observe people carefully and take into account the many causes which can affect how people behave.

The benefits of understanding behaviour are that:

- You become more objective in your observations.
- You are more tolerant of people.
- You get more from people by demonstrating your understanding.
- You help others to understand themselves.
- You gain a better understanding of yourself.

If you make the effort to understand behaviour, you will find it very much easier to manage your own life and get on better with other people.

Knowing more about the origins of behaviour allows you to understand that when people do not behave like themselves there is probably a very good reason, and that when they do not behave like you, they are simply behaving like themselves.

Glossary

Here are some definitions in relation to Understanding Behaviour.

Anxiety – A lurking dread that something nasty is waiting to happen.

Behaviour – The way people experiment to find out how they can function in the world.

Circumstances – The usual scapegoat for unwarranted behaviour.

Conditioning – Having your responses shaped by external influences.

Coping – Dealing successfully with difficult behaviour, even if to do so you decide to do nothing.

Depression – A feeling of being in a dark tunnel with no light at the end.

Experience – The stock-piling of knowledge learned from living.

Nature – The inherited characteristics you are endowed and/or lumbered with.

Need – The plight of constantly wanting something and not necessarily knowing what it is you want.

Nurture – The nourishment you get (or do not get) in your development, rather more significant in earlier life than later.

Personality – The distinctive thoughts, emotions, and qualities that define you as a unique individual.

Reinforcement – The act of strengthening certain responses.

Role-playing – Behaviour which always results in bad feeling as the denouement.

Self-fulfilling prophecy – The expectation that a certain thing is inevitable, which usually makes it so.

Signs – Obvious indicators that something is wrong, providing you notice them.

Stress – Mental tension resulting in an inability to cope, and made worse by that inability.

Trauma – State of shock dramatic enough to cause long-lasting effects.

Understanding – Gaining as much insight as possible, in as many dimensions as possible.

Victim – One who feels that life always favours other people.

Victor – One who feels compelled to come out on top.

The Author

Kate Keenan is a Chartered Occupational Psychologist with degrees in affiliated subjects (B.Sc., M.Phil.) and a number of qualifications in others.

She founded Keenan Research, an industrial psychology consultancy, in 1978. The work of the consultancy is fundamentally concerned with helping people to achieve their potential and make a better job of their management.

By devising work programmes for companies she enables them to target and remedy their managerial problems – from personnel selection and individual assessment to team building and attitude surveys. She believes in giving priority to training the managers to institute their own programmes, so that their company resources are developed and expanded.

She enjoys detecting behavioural clues but admits that it is not always easy to understand what they signify. She never fails to be surprised by the diversity and range of human behaviour in its many and unexpected manifestations. She even surprises herself about her own.